IN THE QUIET,SHE STAYED

FOR YOU, WITH ALL THE WORDS I NEVER SAID

CHETAN KUMAR KORIVI

To the one who stayed —
not because you had to,
but because you wanted to.

You are not my sister by blood,
but the soul I chose in a world that often didn't make sense.

This is for the moments you didn't know saved me.
This is for you.

Contents

Foreword

I never planned to write a book.

This wasn't born out of ambition or the desire to be seen — it came from something far more raw. This book began in the quiet moments of reflection, after a long line of heartbreaks, mistakes, and mental battles that left me unsure of who I was becoming. Somewhere in the middle of that mess, she appeared — not like a savior, not like a miracle — but like a calm presence that asked for nothing and gave everything.

She wasn't someone I searched for.
She was someone life gently handed to me, after all the noise had quieted.

I often found it difficult to express what I felt. Sometimes, I still do. But with her, things felt safe — my thoughts, my silence, my scars. And in that safety, I found healing. I found a version of myself I thought was lost.

This book isn't fiction. It's not polished with plot twists or clever metaphors. It's honest. It's real. It's pages filled with memories, reflections, quiet heartbreak, and loud gratitude — all for the one person who reminded me that I was never truly alone.

If you're holding this in your hands, you're holding a chapter of my life that changed everything.

Thank you for reading.
Thank you for witnessing.

Preface

They say we all carry a story, and most of us carry it in silence. Mine was a mixture of blurred memories, unrealized emotions, and long pauses between what I felt and what I could say.

This book is my voice — the one that trembled, the one that stayed quiet for too long, the one that finally found the courage to speak.

After my world cracked open — emotionally, mentally — I didn't expect anyone to stay. I was dealing with confusion, heartbreak, and the weight of feeling misunderstood, even by the people closest to me. And yet, in the middle of that chaos, she sat beside me. Not to fix me. Not to label me. But to just be there — fully, completely, and without fear.

That kind of presence... it changes you. It teaches you that healing isn't loud. It's soft, patient, consistent — like the way she listened, or laughed, or simply stayed up late talking to me under the balcony lights.

This book is not a grand literary piece. It's not about perfection. It's a conversation. A thank-you. A memory carved into paper. It's for her, yes. But it's also for anyone who has ever been saved quietly.

If you've ever found someone who made you feel safe in your most unsafe moments — someone who didn't leave when it would've been easier — this book is for you too.

Acknowledgements

Writing this book has been a journey through my heart, and I couldn't have reached this point without the support of some very special people.

First and foremost, to Charmisha - the sister I chose, the one who stood by me when the world seemed heavy and confusing. Your kindness, understanding, and quiet strength gave me hope when I had none. You didn't just listen; you truly heard me. This book is a small way to say thank you for being my anchor and my inspiration.

To my family, thank you for your love and patience even when I struggled to express myself. Though we sometimes didn't understand each other fully, your presence has always meant the world to me.

To my friends, who reminded me that I am never alone even in my darkest moments your support kept me going.

And to anyone reading this who has faced their own battles or felt misunderstood — may you find comfort in these pages, and know that you are not alone.

This is my first book — more like pouring all my feelings out, this time for someone I didn't end up losing completely... but with a happy ending.

Thank you for being part of this journey with me.

Prologue

Before her, I thought I had to keep everything inside.

I used to sit in crowded rooms and still feel like a ghost. I laughed at jokes that didn't land in my heart, nodded through conversations I couldn't follow, and smiled just enough to keep the questions away. People looked at me, but no one really saw.

Then came the silence — the kind that follows a breakup, a diagnosis, and the realization that your own mind has turned into something you no longer understand. Psychosis. A word heavy enough to shatter your image of yourself. I didn't know how to carry it. I didn't even want to.

I went to her house just to escape for a few days — nothing planned, nothing special. But the moment I heard her footsteps behind me, playfully trying to scare me, I knew: something was about to change.

Not in a dramatic, cinematic way.
In a quiet way.
The way she sat beside me.
The way she listened without flinching.
The way her eyes never changed, even when I showed her the parts of myself I had hidden from everyone.

This isn't a love story in the way movies tell it.
It's a story of choosing someone. Of being chosen.
Of healing, in the most unexpected arms.

This book starts here —
With a balcony, a bottle of water, and the words:
"You are the purest soul I have ever met... I wish I could adopt you."

For Her

I don't remember the exact moment she walked into my life.
Maybe that's the thing about people who are meant to stay—they
don't arrive with fireworks. They arrive with calm. And she was
calm. Not loud, not flashy—just the kind of warmth I never knew I
needed.
For Her, With All the Words I Never Said

CHAPTER ONE

THE DAY I WAITED

"Some people walk into your life quietly—and stay louder than your thoughts."

I arrived early that morning—not too early to seem eager, but not too late to seem careless either. The truth was, I didn't know why I was so nervous. Maybe it was because I hadn't seen her in a while. Maybe it was because a part of me believed that just being in her presence could fix something inside me.

She wasn't home. She had left for work before I arrived. The house was calm, sunlight slipping through the old curtains, casting sleepy shadows on the walls. Her brother was kind, casual, engaging enough to keep the day from feeling too slow, but my mind wasn't really in the room. It was in the streets outside, counting the hours, wondering if she was thinking of me too.

I waited.

I had no expectations. I didn't come with a plan or a speech or even a gift. I came with a broken heart, fragile thoughts, and memories that wouldn't let go. I had just stepped out of a relationship that left me unsure of myself—unsure if I was lovable, stable, normal even. Words like psychosis had been thrown at me, and they clung to my skin like wet clothes. Heavy. Shameful.

Misunderstood.

No one had explained it to me clearly. No one had asked how I felt about it. Everyone just... reacted.

But she didn't.

She never had to say much. Her presence alone was the kind of silence that spoke louder than a room full of noise.

That evening, I was talking with her brother in the bedroom, half lost in my thoughts, half scrolling through nothing on my phone. The lights were soft. The house felt fuller with night approaching. Then—without warning—someone crept up behind me.

"Boo!"

She whispered it just standing behind me, like a child trying to spook an adult but knowing she'd laugh before I would.

I turned, startled—but not afraid. For the first time in weeks, maybe months, I felt something bright inside me click back into place.

Her eyes were lit with mischief, her hair still slightly messy from work, and her laugh—that laugh—was the sound of relief. Not the "Did I scare you?" laugh. No. It was the "I'm happy to see you again" kind. Unspoken. Pure.

I smiled, probably wider than I meant to. She looked at me with that half-playful, half-knowing look she always had.

"You're finally here," she said.

We spent the evening talking about everything and nothing. She teased me. I smiled more than I wanted to admit. But beneath all the laughter, there was something deeper moving quietly between us—like two hearts learning to recognize the same beat.

What shocked me most wasn't just how happy I was to see her. It was how safe I felt around her.

She asked questions without judgement. She listened without interrupting. She understood without needing explanations.

Even when I stumbled while speaking, even when I paused mid-sentence because the thoughts in my head were too loud—she waited. Not with pity. Not with pressure. Just with presence.

I remember watching her that night from the corner of my eye as she laughed at something silly I said. And for a moment, I thought,

This... this is the version of me I forgot existed.

The one who laughed, the one who didn't overthink every move, the one who didn't feel broken.

She brought that out of me without trying.

And that's how I knew—

She was more than just a sister.

She was the calm in my storm.

CHAPTER TWO

THE BALCONY CONFESSION

"Some people don't ask to be let in. They simply barge—and make a home out of you."

It wasn't planned.

No one said, "Let's talk all night."

No camera rolled, no music played in the background, no grand cinematic setup. Just the night, the stars above us, the dim streetlight below, and two people who had more to say than they knew.

It was past midnight when we stepped out onto the balcony. The city was asleep, or pretending to be. The wind was soft, brushing gently past the metal railing. Somewhere in the distance, a dog barked once and then fell silent. But up there—it was just us.

She sat beside me.

Not too close.

Not too far.

Exactly where she always sat in my life—close enough to be felt, but never overwhelming.

She looked at the sky, not me.

And maybe that's why I found the courage to speak.

"I've never told anyone this," I said, my voice quieter than usual.

She didn't turn.

Didn't say "Tell me."

She just... listened. Like she already knew the words before I did.

"I never touch anyone without asking," I said to myself. "Even if they're just friends. Even if it's just a shoulder tap. I don't know, I just... I don't want to break the invisible space people build around themselves."

She turned slightly now, not surprised, not confused—just soft.

And still silent.

"But that night," I whispered, "when we were sitting here... I didn't want permission. Not in a bad way. Just... in a way that felt like I had known you for years. Like this closeness didn't need language anymore."

She smiled. Not the teasing one.

The real one. The rare one.

The one that says I know exactly what you mean, and you're not weird for feeling it.

"I felt it too," she said, like it was the most normal thing in the world.

And yet, it broke something open in me.

We sat there, our arms slightly brushing as we leaned against the railing.

I remember every second of that silence.

Every flutter of the wind.

Every blink of the streetlight.

Every heartbeat that said more than words could.

I wanted to tell her everything then.

That she was the only person who could see past the noise in my head.

That she didn't just make me feel normal—she made me feel seen.

That she wasn't just someone I admired—she was someone I trusted with the most chaotic corners of my soul.

We didn't kiss.

We didn't even hold hands.

But I swear, that night was more intimate than any physical touch could ever be.

It was the night I saw love—not as romance, not as drama, not as obsession.

But as stillness. As peace. As knowing someone and still choosing them—again and again.

And just before we went back inside, she did something I'll never forget.

She reached out and tucked a strand of hair behind her ear, nervously, and then looked at me with that tiny smirk.

"You overthink too much for others," she said.

"But I like that you do."

I smiled.

For the first time in years, I wasn't afraid of being too much.

Because to her—I was just enough.

CHAPTER THREE

SHE TOOK MY NIGHTMARES, TOO

"Some people don't just stay through your chaos—they sit beside it and hold your hand until it stops shaking."

It was never about the ghosts in my sleep.

Not really.

It was about what they reminded me of:

the people I lost,

the voices that never left,

the thoughts I tried to silence,

and the guilt of being too much for the world to understand.

There was one night—worse than the others.

I had woken up drenched in sweat.

Heart pounding.

No air.

No words.

Just the echo of something that wasn't even real... but felt more alive than me.

I sat on the edge of the bed.

Fingers trembling.

Eyes fixed on the floor, like I could ground myself through the granite tiles.

And then she warmed me with through text messages.

I can feel her making me feel

Softly.

Three gentle taps .

Like even the sound of her entering my world knew how to be kind.

As if she stepped in with a sleepy face, hair tied back, eyes barely open.

"You okay?"

That's all she asked.

Not "What happened?"

Not "Why are you like this?"

Just—you okay?

I couldn't lie.

Not to her.

Not when she asked at me like she actually wanted to hear the truth.

"No," I said, my voice cracking. "Not really."

She didn't gasp.

Didn't panic.

Didn't treat me like something broken.

She just walked over, sat beside me, and handed me a water bottle.

"You are the purest soul I have ever met.. I wish i could adopt you," she said.

And in that one sentence, she gave me a kind of belonging I didn't even know I was searching for.

She didn't just stay.

She became the calm inside the storm.

We didn't talk much.

Sometimes, she told me the most random stories from her office.

Sometimes, she just sat there, letting the silence between us be the comfort I didn't know I needed.

She even joked once.
"should have used sleeping pills unnoticed in the water."
I smiled. Genuinely.
It was the first time I had smiled after a nightmare.
Over time, the nightmares didn't stop.
But they became... softer.
Less sharp.
Less terrifying.
Because now, when I woke up sweating,
I remembered the girl who once sat beside me in the dark
and made it feel like morning.
And the strangest thing?
She never treated it like a favor.
She never said "Look at what I did for you."
She just... did it.
Because that's who she is.
She didn't fight my monsters.
She sat beside them,
unafraid,
until they got tired of trying to scare me.

SELFIES AND SOFT SMILES

"Some memories are not loud. They don't scream or demand attention. They live quietly in the folds of our gallery, under the soft light of trust."

It wasn't a planned photo shoot.

No makeup, no perfect lighting, no angles.

Just us.

A phone held between two lives that had somehow found their way to each other,

not through blood or fate,

but through something even rarer—understanding.

She said,

"Let's take one, we haven't yet."

I hesitated. I always do.

I don't like how I look in pictures.

Too tired. Too raw.

Like the weight behind my smile might show.

But with her, that fear faded.

Because she never waited for the perfect me.

She liked the honest one.
We stood by the window—light brushing her face.
I held the phone, arms stretched.
She leaned in.
So close, but not in a way that invaded.
Just... fit.
Snap.
Another.
A funny face.
Another.
My signature move (Thumbs up for no reason).
Then just... a quiet smile.
The kind of smile you only give to someone who knows the parts of you that tremble—and still stays.
I looked at the photos later that night, when I couldn't sleep.
And for once, I didn't hate what I saw.
I saw two people who looked real.
No masks.
No filters.
Her smile wasn't for the camera—it was for me.
Mine wasn't forced—it was because of her.
Sometimes, people click photos to remember the moment.
But sometimes, people click photos because the moment is worth saving.
Because you know that someday, when life gets heavier again, you'll need something to look at and say—
"Yes. That happened. She was there. I was okay."
The next day, she laughed looking at one of them.
"God, we look like cousins who've survived an apocalypse."
I chuckled. "We kinda have."
She paused.
Nodded.
And looked at me in that way again—like she knew what I meant, even when I didn't say it out loud.
You don't need 1000 photos to prove a bond.

Sometimes, one blurry selfie with the right person
is worth more than an entire album with people who don't know
your soul.
And this one?
This one will always be mine.

CHAPTER FIVE

She Was the Home I Didn't Know I Missed

"Home is not a place. It's the feeling of being understood without explanation."

I've been in many houses.
Walls with photographs.
Rooms full of people.
Laughter echoing from the kitchen.
But none of them ever felt like they were mine.
You see, when you live in your own head too much,
when your thoughts are louder than your voice,
it doesn't matter how soft the bedsheets are,
or how many welcome signs hang near the door—
you still feel like a guest.
And then I stayed in her house.
Not for a day. Not as a visitor.
But as someone who lingered—

and slowly realized I didn't want to leave.
It started with small things.
The way she'd call out from the kitchen,
"Do you want chai?"
Like it wasn't even a question.
Like she already knew the answer.
The way her brother laughed when I made dumb jokes,
and she rolled her eyes like I was a fool she'd still defend if needed.
The way her room felt like it remembered people.
Not just housed them.
We sat on the floor one evening,
legs stretched,
her hands holding a light novel, mine tracing random lines on the tiles.
"You think you'll be okay?" she asked.
I didn't answer right away.
Instead, I looked around her house.
At the warmth.
At her presence.
At the stillness that made me forget my chaos.
And I said—"Here, yes."
I didn't know I was missing something.
Not until I stopped waking up with panic.
Not until I started laughing without flinching.
Not until I heard her footsteps in the hall and felt... calm.
She wasn't loud comfort.
She was soft space.
The kind you don't notice until you leave
and feel the emptiness wrap around you like cold air.
One night, I told her,
"I think I found my home."
She tilted her head. "Where?"
I looked at her.
Not the house.

Not the walls.
Her.
And she didn't smile or cry or say something dramatic.
She just nodded.
Like she already knew.
I don't know what will happen tomorrow.
Where life will throw us.
What cities, what stories.
But I know this—
Even if I end up on the other side of the world,
with no house, no map, no name—
If she's around,
I'll find my way.
Because she was the first person who made me feel like I belonged
without asking me to change.

CHAPTER SIX

The Night I Almost Told Her Everything

"Sometimes the hardest words to say are the ones that mean the most."

The night was quiet, the kind that folds you in and makes the world pause.

We sat side by side on the balcony, the cool breeze carrying whispers of things we never said aloud.

I watched her face in the dim light.. soft, kind, a little tired but still full of that spark that made me want to speak my soul.

I wanted to tell her everything.

How she was more than a friend, more than family.

How she saved me when I thought I was lost.

How her presence quieted the chaos inside me.

But the words stuck like a knot in my throat.

I was scared—scared she wouldn't understand, scared I'd lose her if I crossed that line.

Instead, I talked about small things.

About how I always wanted permission before touching anyone—even a friend.

How trust meant more than anything.

She smiled, a little curious, but patient.

She didn't push.

She let me take my time.

That night, I realized love isn't always about grand declarations.

Sometimes it's in the silence.

In the way she looked at me without judgment.

In the way she stayed even when I didn't say a word.

We took some starings at city in silence,

her laughter breaking the stillness,

my smile softer than before.

She said, "You're different since i first met you."

And I knew it was because of her.

I never told her how close I came to saying it all.

But maybe one day, I will.

For now, this is enough:

Knowing she's the one who understands,

the one who stays,

the one who makes me better.

the one who reads this book maybe it will reach her.

CHAPTER SEVEN

WHEN I THOUGHT I COULD LOSE HER

"Some storms don't come with thunder, just a silence that breaks everything inside you."

I didn't expect the news.

It came like a soft whisper with the weight of a thousand screams:

"She might be getting married."

I smiled when I heard it.

That fake kind of smile you wear when your chest is collapsing, but you still want to seem okay.

"Good for her," I said.

But inside, I was already rewriting every memory.

I thought of the balcony talks.

The late-night tea.

The way she called me out when I overthought.

The selfies.

The small jokes only we got.

And in that moment,

I realized I wasn't ready to let go.

Not like this.
Not to someone who hadn't seen her the way I had.
I knew I had no right.
She wasn't mine.
She never promised anything beyond what we were.
But still—
It felt like the universe was taking back something
I didn't even know I'd built my healing around.
For the first time in a long time,
I sat quietly with my pain.
Not angry.
Not broken.
Just...
Empty.
Like the part of me that had started to feel whole
was slowly fading back into its cracks.
I didn't tell her.
Didn't ask.
Didn't confess.
What could I say?
"Please don't go"?
"Please don't belong to someone else"?
She deserved joy.
Even if it didn't include me the way I wished it would.
That night, I wrote something in my notes app:
"If you ever walk away,
please leave behind the version of me
you helped build.
I'll take care of him.
I promise." - yeah i know this is too much but it made sense at
the moment.

CHAPTER EIGHT

THE UNSAID THINGS I'LL ALWAYS CARRY

"Some stories are never told.. not because they don't matter, but because they matter too much."

There are things I never said out loud.
Maybe because I couldn't.
Maybe because I knew saying them would change everything.
But they're here —
tucked in the corners of memories,
in quiet glances,
and long silences after you smiled at me.
You never asked me to love you.
You never owed me anything.
And I never wanted to burden you with my feelings.
Because what we had... it was perfect in its own way.
I wasn't ready to risk that.
Still, I carry these words.
I carry them when I hear your voice after days.
When your name flashes on my phone and my heart remembers how to beat softer.

I carry them when I see your wedding plans and I pretend I'm just a friend watching from the crowd.

I carry the moment you stood next to me on that balcony,

not realizing you were the first person in years I didn't want to run from.

I carry the way you understood my silence better than anyone understood my words.

I carry the way you looked at me—

not as someone broken,

but someone healing.

Sometimes, I wonder if you knew.

Sometimes, I hope you didn't.

Because if you did and stayed silent,

that hurts more than never knowing.

But maybe this was our story—

one of silent love,

of unsaid goodbyes,

of "what if" stitched between real moments.

So I'll carry it.

All of it.

For as long as I live.

Not because I didn't have the courage to tell you...

but because loving you, even in silence,

was still better than anything I ever had.

CHAPTER NINE

IF THIS IS GOODBYE, LET IT BE GENTLE

"Some people don't leave your life. They become part of how you live it."

I don't know if this is goodbye.

Maybe you'll stay.

Maybe you'll drift.

Maybe life will place miles and marriages and memories between us.

But if this is goodbye...

I don't want it to be bitter.

You weren't a chapter.

You were the turning point.

The moment the story changed,

the reason I found color again

after years of grayscale.

You weren't just someone I loved —

you were someone who taught me how to love.

Gently.

Silently.

Completely.
So, no.. I won't hold on with resentment.
I won't curse fate.
I won't ask "why not me?"
Because what you gave me —
even if it ends here —
was more than I thought I'd ever have.
If you walk away,
I will follow your footsteps to my limit.
But I'll stand a moment longer,
watching the shape of you fade into the future,
whispering thank you into the wind.
Because you didn't just enter my life —
you anchored it.
I'll keep our memories like pages in a book I never stop rereading.
Not to get stuck in the past,
but to remember who I became because of you.
You helped me write the best version of myself.
And I will carry that version forward,
even if you're not beside me anymore.
So if this is goodbye,
let it be gentle.
No tears, no regrets.
Only gratitude.
Because you were the calm in my storm,
the smile in my silence,
and the light I never knew I needed.

CHAPTER TEN

You'll Always Be a Part of My Story

"Not every person you love becomes your partner. Some become your purpose, your peace, your poetry."

I used to think people were either in your life forever,
or they left completely.
But I was wrong.
Some people live in your pauses,
your playlists,
your quietest thoughts.
They stay, even when they're gone.
You will always be a part of my story.
Not because I didn't move on,
but because I didn't want to erase you to heal.
You were never a mistake.
You were a miracle in motion —
the kind that came when I needed saving,
not in grand gestures,
but in small moments that felt like home.
When I tell my story someday —

maybe to a stranger,
or to someone who loves me differently —
I'll talk about you like a whisper.
Like a chapter too sacred to say aloud.
But one that shaped the entire plot.
You were the reason I started believing again.
Not just in love...
but in being loved.
You showed me I could be held without being judged,
heard without being fixed,
and known without having to explain.
Even now, when I wake from the occasional nightmare,
your voice is still the one that calms the storm.
Even if it's just a memory now.
And when I see the world with less fear than before,
it's because you taught me not to run from my mind
but walk beside it, gently.
So yes —
You'll always be a part of my story.
Not as someone I lost,
but as someone who left a light in my darkness.
Not every story ends with together.
But every real one leaves behind a forever.

CHAPTER ELEVEN

LETTERS I NEVER SENT YOU

"I wrote to you, even when I couldn't speak. Because some truths belong to paper, not people."

Letter 1:

On the night we stayed up talking...
   You remember that night?
   The moon was too full.
   The wind was soft.
   And I, for once, didn't feel like I was drowning.
   I didn't tell you then,
   but I think that was the first time in years
   that I felt safe.
   You didn't save me..
   you reminded me I could still save myself.
   That night, I slept without fear.
   And woke up wanting to live again.

Letter 2:

After you smiled at my scars, not my stories...
    You didn't look away.
    You didn't flinch.
    When I spoke about my past,
    when I broke mid-sentence,
    you simply said,
    "That must have been heavy."
    And suddenly,
    I wasn't ashamed of carrying it anymore.

Letter 3:

When I learned about your engagement...
    I smiled. I really did.
    Because you looked happy.
    And if love means anything,
    it means wanting you to be happy,
    even if it's not with me.
    Still, that night, I felt something down for the version of us
    that only existed in my hopes.
    I buried that version gently.
    And whispered goodbye
    to the dream
    I never dared speak aloud.

Letter 4:

For the future you'll live without me...
    I hope he understands your silence.
    I hope he makes you laugh like you made me laugh.
    I hope he doesn't need to be told
    that your favorite color changes with your mood,
    or that you fake being strong

just to hold everyone else together.
I hope he earns you,
not just loves you.
Because you're not just someone to keep —
you're someone to grow with.
And if he doesn't see that,
he didn't deserve you in the first place.

Letter 5:

That I wrote... but can never give you.
    You were the person I wanted to tell everything to.
    And the one I knew I never should.
    So I'm telling this book instead.
    Because paper listens without judgment.
    And ink doesn't walk away.

CHAPTER TWELVE

I Never Told You, But You Saved Me

*"Not by doing something heroic, but by staying when I
thought no one would."*

I don't think you ever realized it.
You thought you were just being yourself.
But to me,
you were a reason.
A reason to fight through the fog.
A reason to breathe on days that felt like drowning.
A reason to believe that maybe,
just maybe,
I was not broken beyond repair.
You didn't fix me.
You didn't give advice.
You didn't try to change me.
You stayed.
And sometimes, staying
is the bravest thing someone can do for another.
You sat beside me in silence,

not because you were uncomfortable —
but because you respected my storm.
You listened,
not to reply,
but to understand.
And that?
That was everything.
You never asked me to explain why I was the way I was.
You never labeled me.
You never said, "Get over it."
Instead, you said:
"I'm here."
"I get it."
"Do it"
"Text her"
"Don't regret"
"Let's go look at the stars."
That night on the balcony —
the wind was cold,
but your presence was warmth.
I didn't need to say I was tired.
You knew.
I didn't ask for comfort.
But you wrapped it around me anyway,
like a blanket of unspoken empathy.
So yes —
You saved me.
Not like in the movies.
Not with grand rescues.
But with your laughter,
your kindness,
your ordinary magic.
You saved me just by existing.
I hope one day you read this.
Maybe after years,

maybe when the world is quieter.
And you realize you were someone's miracle,
without even trying to be.

CHAPTER THIRTEEN

IF THIS IS GOODBYE... I'LL STILL BE GRATEFUL

"Some people don't stay in your life forever, but they stay in your soul... always."

If this is where the road ends,
If life takes us in different directions,
If our conversations fade to memories,
I want you to know... I'm still grateful.
Grateful for the time we had.
Grateful for the moments you stayed.
Grateful for the version of me
you helped bring back to life.
There are people who enter your world with noise —
and leave you with silence.
You weren't one of them.
You entered gently.
You stayed calmly.

You left peace behind.
And even if I never hear from you again,
I'll smile whenever I think of you.
I may never be the person who holds your hand
at the end of the day.
But I was lucky enough
to be the person who held your trust
for a little while.
And I don't take that lightly.
I won't write poems with your name anymore.
I won't look at the moon and whisper what-ifs.
But I'll carry a soft place in my heart
where your laughter still echoes,
your words still comfort,
and your memory still smiles.
If this is goodbye —
let it be beautiful.
Let it be thankful.
Let it be soft.
Because you were one of the best things
to ever happen to me.
And goodbye doesn't change that.

CHAPTER FOURTEEN

A Page I Leave Blank... For You

"Some love doesn't need punctuation. It breathes in the space between words."

This chapter has no lines.
No paragraphs.
No explanations.
Just white space.
Just silence.
Just you.
Because I realized something:
Every time I tried to capture you in words,
I reduced you.
You are not ink.
You are not letters.
You are everything I never learned how to write.
So I leave this page blank..
like how you showed up when I stopped explaining.
Like how you understood what I couldn't say.
Like how you saw me

even when I couldn't look at myself.
This page is for the moments
that happened in silence.
The smiles between sentences.
The breath before confession.
The pause where hearts spoke.
You are this chapter.
Not in what I wrote,
but in what I couldn't.

CHAPTER FIFTEEN

FOR YOU

For You – My Answer To You

*"Special Edition - kinda overact right? special edition! , can't blame me... this is my first time bleh *pulling tongue out to make fun of you*."*

I always wondered why you once said,
"I think you're more mature than anyone else your age."
Back then, I smiled and shrugged.
But inside, I doubted it.
Me? Mature? Are you kidding?
Now, after all this, I think I have an answer.
Or at least... an opinion.
You know how it's always the biggest idiots
who give the wisest advice?
Not because they're wise —
but because they already did the dumb stuff,
faced the worst consequences,
and survived it.
So maybe... that's me.
I've done the dumbest things.
Made the worst choices.
Jumped when I should've waited.
Trusted when I should've healed.
Stayed silent when I should've screamed.
And yet.. here I am.
Still standing.
Still learning.
Still loving people like you
with everything I have left.
So maybe that's why I seem mature to you.
Because I messed up enough to know
what really matters.

And it's not pride.
Not ego.
Not perfection.
It's honesty.
It's staying kind even after pain.
It's still choosing to care when the world says "don't."
So thank you..
for thinking the best of me,
even when I couldn't see it myself.
Now you know the secret:
It's not maturity.
It's just... the wisdom of a beautiful idiot
who got lucky enough to meet you.

Epilogue

One Last Look Back

"Some people are not chapters. They are the spine of the whole book."

Years will pass.
    Photos will fade.
    New names will enter our contact lists,
    new places will hold our routines.
    But on some quiet evening,
    when the world softens —
    I'll think of you.
    And I'll smile.
    Not because I miss you with pain,
    but because I remember you with peace.
    Because even if we don't talk anymore,
    even if life writes us into different novels,
    you were a chapter I never wanted to end.
    You were never just someone I knew.
    You were the one who saw me when I was invisible.
    Who spoke when I had no voice left.
    Who stayed when I was hard to love.
    I might see your wedding photos someday,
    I might hear about your children,
    your milestones, your travels.
    And I won't break.
    I won't cry.
    I'll just whisper inside,

"She deserved every bit of that joy."
Because you do.
If this story ever finds you again,
I hope you read it with warmth,
not pity, not sadness,
just the knowing smile
that once, someone wrote a whole book
because they were lucky enough
to be loved by you.